A Simple Christmas

A Simple Christmas

Celebrating the Old-Fashioned Way in a Post-Modern World

Lori Salkin and Rob Sperry

**Andrews McMeel
Publishing**

Kansas City

To both of our mothers,
who lent us their names and who are the ones
who really make the holidays happen.

www.andrewsmcmeel.com

Library of Congress Cataloging-in-Publication Data
Salkin, Lori.
  A simple Christmas : celebrating the old-fashioned way in a post-modern world / Lori Salkin and Rob Sperry.
     p.   cm.
   ISBN 0-8362-3593-2 (hd)
   1. Christmas. 2. Simplicity (Philosophy) I. Sperry, Rob.
II. Title.
GT4985.S16   1997
394.2663—dc21   97-14356
                                                          CIP

Book design and composition by Top Dog Design
Illustration by Matthew Taylor

ATTENTION: SCHOOLS AND BUSINESSES

Andrews McMeel books are available at quantity discounts with bulk purchase for educational, business, or sales promotional use. For information, please write to: Special Sales Department, Andrews McMeel Publishing, 4520 Main Street, Kansas City, Missouri 64111.

Introduction

Christmas! Roasting chestnuts over an open fire, reindeer gliding through a starry sky, stealing kisses under the mistletoe. It's everyone's favorite time of year, when the air is crisp and the nights sparkle with anticipation.

We keep busy wrapping gifts and baking gingerbread, and sometimes in our rush to make this holiday perfect for our family and our friends, we forget what Christmas really means. We go shopping to try and find the right gift for each person on our list and come home tired, cranky, and hating all mankind—from the disinterested clerks who take our money without even a "thank you" to the rude and frenzied shoppers who push past us and grab whatever they can get their hands on. It's enough to make you want to say, "Bah, humbug!" In an effort to avoid setting foot in the mall between Thanksgiving and Christmas Day, some of us try shopping even earlier, before we even *feel* like Christmas is coming. What's the fun in shopping for presents when you aren't ready to think about the occasion?

Then, suddenly, it's over. You're exhausted from

cooking all those holiday meals, and the house is a mess—littered with ribbon and bits of paper that are the only remnants of the hours of wrapping the week before. A new toy is already broken, there's a football game blaring from the television set, and someone isn't feeling well and needs your special care. In a couple of weeks, the first credit card bills will arrive. These are the ones that you're afraid to open, since you've overspent again in that last-ditch effort to finish the gift buying! Where's your Christmas spirit now?

We know where it is. It's in the warmth of a crackling fireplace against your back. It's in the faces of people bathed in candlelight at midnight Mass. It's in the shining eyes of children as they hang their stockings on Christmas Eve. It's in the hushed silence of a darkened room, illuminated only with the twinkling lights on the Christmas tree. It's in your heart, as you embrace your family and friends and welcome them to your home. It's in the celebration of an old-fashioned Christmas, as it was before the world became so high-tech and overcommercialized.

A Simple Christmas is a collection of short essays that depict ways to celebrate the kind of old-fashioned

Christmas that we all long for, but seem to forget about year after year. It offers suggestions for getting back to the basics of Christmas, so that the spirit behind the holiday can shine through. *A Simple Christmas* won't tell you how to get through the holiday more efficiently, and it won't tell you to forego presents or not to trim the tree. But it *will* help you rediscover the values and traditions of less complicated times, which are still as relevant today as they were hundreds of years ago. Celebrating a simpler Christmas means feeling happier, more fulfilled, and discovering that, despite all the commercialization and bustle of today, this holiday need never lose its meaning.

Help an elderly person buy and decorate a Christmas tree

Sometimes it can be easy to overlook someone's physical problems, especially when those frailties do not seem overwhelming. But many elderly people have a hard time managing to buy a Christmas tree and bring it home, much less decorate it as they have in years past. If you know someone, a relative or neighbor, who may have trouble putting up a tree, offer to help her buy and trim her Christmas tree. When someone lives alone, it can seem like too much of an effort to have a tree, but if you share this special tradition with her, you're sharing more than your time and energy—you're sharing the spirit of Christmas.

Remember that if someone has trouble putting up a tree, she will also have trouble taking it down after the holiday. Don't forget to visit after Christmas is over to help your elderly friend pack away ornaments. Dispose of the tree for her, and help clean up any stray pine needles. This can become a new holiday tradition.

Donate an old winter coat or a warm blanket to a homeless shelter

If you're like most people, your closets are filled with clothes and linens that you never wear or use. It doesn't matter what you give at Christmas, just as long as you think of another person's needs. Donate those old winter coats, big sweaters, or warm blankets to a homeless shelter or other charitable organization in your neighborhood. Wrap a handful of Christmas cookies in plastic wrap and tuck it into the pocket of the coat. Once its new owner claims it, she will get a sweet surprise. Let your children give away some of their own clothes so they can share in the spirit of the holiday.

Spend more time with God

Most people we talked to wanted their Christmases to be more spiritual. Yet they don't spend much time in church or doing anything that would help them feel spiritually connected. In the midst of shopping frenzy, a church will seem even calmer, quieter, and more peaceful than usual. Even a few minutes inside a local church will be restorative for your mind and your soul.

Serve hot toddies to your guests

Hot toddies are traditional drinks served during the holidays to warm the body as well as the spirit. Since there is a quarter cup of Scotch in each drink, these are really for adults only. You can make a delicious, hot, nonalcoholic raspberry hot chocolate for children and anyone else who wants to avoid the alcohol by putting some raspberry syrup in a mug before adding the chocolate.

HOT TODDY RECIPE
Serves eight
Ingredients:
32 whole cloves
2 lemons, cut into quarters
16 teaspoons sugar
2 cups Scotch whisky
8 cinnamon sticks
4 tablespoons butter
boiling water

Directions:
Stud each lemon quarter with 4 cloves, and place each piece of lemon into an 8-ounce mug. Add 2 teaspoons sugar, $^1/_4$ cup of Scotch and $^1/_2$ tablespoon butter to each mug. Fill mugs with boiling water. Serve immediately, using the cinnamon sticks as stirrers to add flavor.

Never give fruitcakes!

This is our only rule: Never give away a fruitcake unless you make it yourself! It's a cliché already that the same fruitcakes continue to circle the globe each year, merely changing hands and never being eaten. Avoid becoming the brunt of countless jokes and forget the fruitcake.

Avoid using credit cards

In order to avoid January's bill-paying hangover and high interest rates, don't charge holiday gifts on your credit cards. A good rule of thumb to keep in mind is, if you can't afford to pay cash, you probably can't afford it. Pull out last year's credit card statements and assess the damage. How long did it take you to pay off your Christmas debts? Three months? The problem with credit cards is that they don't give you a true sense of how much money you have actually spent. Credit counselors suggest that your December budget shouldn't exceed your normal monthly expenditures by more than 40 percent. It's always better to save a little in October and November so that you're not hit so hard in January.

Invite someone who has no family nearby to celebrate Christmas with your family

Not everyone is able to celebrate Christmas with their families—and chances are you know someone like this, whether she is a co-worker, a neighbor, or simply an acquaintance. Whether she is elderly, lives far away from her relatives, or doesn't have enough time off, it can be difficult for her to get home. Although they won't admit it, most people don't like to be alone over Christmas. If you suspect that someone you know may be by herself, take the initiative and invite her home to celebrate with your family. A surrogate family's celebration will bring the Christmas spirit into her life.

Have a smaller tree this year

The Christmas tree was first popularized by Queen Victoria and Prince Albert, who placed a small tree on a tabletop and decorated it for the holiday. A tabletop tree is easier to handle, requires fewer ornaments to look lovely, and needs not be placed in an out-of-the-way corner of the room.

This year, instead of buying the tallest tree you can find, choose a beautiful little tree and let your children carry it home and decorate it themselves. This is truly a way to simplify your Christmas and maintain a pretty tradition at the same time.

Shop by mail—but start early!

From the day after Thanksgiving until Christmas Eve, department stores and malls become over-crowded, overheated, and overpriced. Shopping in this kind of environment is sure to sap your Christmas spirit and destroy your happy frame of mind. It's no wonder that shopping by mail has become so popular in recent years. These days there is a catalog for everything: clothing, food, books, and furnishings. There are even catalogs that list all the catalogs! But there is one thing you have to remember when shopping with catalogs: You must do it early because catalog warehouses are frequently out of stock of the most popular items by December. And order early to avoid quick delivery charges.

If catalog shopping seems too newfangled for you to be part of an old-fashioned Christmas, remember that Victorian "wish books" were the forerunners of today's catalogs. The first real catalog was published by Ben Franklin in 1744 and offered over six hundred books for sale. America's oldest mail-order company is Orvis, which was founded in 1856. And Sears sent out its first Christmas catalog in 1933,

though its "wish book" was first published in 1891. By the early 1900s, the Sears catalog was over 1,000 pages long and included everything from farm equipment to clothing to toys to home furnishings. Even though Sears stopped publishing its catalogs a few years ago, mail-order shopping is more popular than ever—and since it's an old tradition in this country, don't feel guilty about simplifying your shopping in this manner!

*But if you must go out to do your
Christmas shopping...*

... make sure you do it on weekday mornings, when crowds are at their thinnest. During December, most malls and department stores stay open late— but that's when everyone else thinks they can get most of their shopping done. Instead, work late one night so you can take off time from work in the morning to do your shopping. Just before Thanksgiving most stores are already on their holiday hours schedules, but most shoppers aren't aware of it yet. This is another good time to shop in peace. Large crowds will add a lot of time—not to mention aggravation—to your shopping expeditions. Avoid them at all costs!

Bring out an album of old photographs

Christmas is a time to remember family and friends who can't be with us. On Christmas Eve or Christmas Day ask everyone to tell a story about a friend or family member. Whether they've moved away or passed on, it's important to remember them during the holidays. Before the season begins, ask friends and family who live far away and won't be able to join you to send copies of their favorite photographs from events of the past year. This way you can all share the important events, even if you couldn't spend them together.

Or use old photos to bring back happy memories. See if you can piece together past Christmases that were special.

Make your gift cards special

Don't leave your gift cards for the night before Christmas; by that time, you're feeling pretty overwhelmed by the holiday and writing them out will seem like just another chore. This year, think about writing your cards to the people who matter most to you before you've even chosen their gift. The card should really be a heartfelt note that tells your friends and family members how special they are to you.

Go on a sleigh ride or do anything that brings you outside on a cool night

Nothing evokes the spirit of Christmas more than bundling up against the elements. It's wintertime, but even if there isn't enough snow for sleigh rides or snowmen, put on your coat or jacket, wrap a scarf around your neck, and get outside into the cool night air. If your aim is to foster Christmas cameraderie, gather family and friends for a long walk on a blustery night.

Give away your Christmas breakfast

In Louisa May Alcott's classic book *Little Women*, the four girls sit down to a lonely Christmas breakfast, since their beloved Marmee has gone away to visit their wounded father in the hospital. Meg, Jo, Beth, and Amy are about to devour their bread, eggs, and meat when they think of a poor family they know. Instead of feeling sorry for themselves, the girls realize that there are other people less fortunate, and they decide to deliver their breakfast to the family who needs it far more than the girls do. Breakfast is bundled into a basket, and the girls go off, all together, to bring warmth and joy to a family they barely know. Watching them devour the good food, the four girls realize the true meaning of Christmas.

This year, instead of sitting down to a holiday meal and overeating, pack it up into a basket and deliver it to a family, a church, a homeless shelter, or another organization that serves meals to the poor. Feed your soul instead of your stomach.

Give children gifts of creativity rather than gifts of commercialization

Children are creative by nature, and parents and adult friends should do all they can to foster this natural instinct. Instead of buying a child a Power Ranger toy or a stuffed Barney or a Barbie doll, give gifts that can be used in new ways over and over again. Children can use crayons, paints, colored pencils, clay, Play-Doh, beads, glitter, construction paper, fabric, and all kinds of other items that are easily found in any craft or hobby store to create unique masterpieces of their own.

In addition to presents for budding artists, other gifts of creativity and imagination include musical instruments (check with the parent first!); computer programs; telescopes, microscopes, and other science projects suitable to their age; kaleidoscopes; and books of any kind. All of these gifts will provide more hours of fun and entertainment than any store-bought cartoon character ever could.

Make an edible tree

Instead of hanging the usual ornaments on your Christmas tree, try using candy canes, strings of popcorn, cranberries, colorful dry cereals, and gingerbread men to decorate this year. You'll create an edible tree that everyone can enjoy.

Pass along a family heritage by giving family heirlooms

Instead of always focusing gift-giving on the latest item available in the mall, utilize the Christmas holiday as a time to pass on cherished family heirlooms. It can be something simple, such as a photograph or a letter, or it can be a piece of jewelry, china, or something else special to your family. Every heirloom has a story behind it, so make sure you give the tale along with the item. This enables younger generations to connect with their ancestors, and it helps them learn their family's particular history.

Volunteer in a soup kitchen on Christmas Eve or Christmas Day

Holidays are an especially hard time for the homeless or the hungry. Instead of sitting at home, take the entire family to a nearby soup kitchen to help serve a holiday meal. Even the most jaded family members (including your teenagers) will soon get caught up in the Christmas spirit, and the holiday will become much more meaningful for everyone.

Have a read-aloud hour or afternoon

This is an activity that you can begin on the first day of your children's Christmas vacation. Many parents read to their kids at bedtime, but instead of reading the same old stories, choose a book or a story that parents will enjoy as much as their children, something that will have special relevance for the holiday season. You can read the traditional Christmas stories, or one of the classics, such as Charles Dickens's *Great Expectations* or *'Twas the Night before Christmas*. It doesn't really matter what you read; it matters that everyone sits down together to listen and share the story. You'll probably find that your kids would rather listen to a story than watch cartoons—and you will get as much out of the experience as they will.

Set an extra place at your holiday table

Every time you set the table for a holiday meal, remember to set an extra place for someone who may need it. You can invite a lonely neighbor, someone you know who doesn't have a family to spend the holiday with, a recent widow or widower, or anyone you may meet who doesn't have a place to go. With a place already set at the table, your guest will instantly feel welcome and at home.

Unplug the television set

Many people complain that much of the Christmas holiday is spent in front of a blaring television. This year take a drastic step and unplug yours. You'll probably encounter some complaining at first, but eventually everyone will learn to get along without "the mind box." You can keep up with the news by reading the paper, and there isn't anything else that is really worth watching when you could be spending those hours with friends or family. Christmas is a time of connection, but when the TV is on, people are in their own little worlds. If you are usually in the kitchen while everyone else is watching a football game, that's an even better reason to hide the remote control: Get the rest of the family to help make the holiday happen.

Adopt a Christmas pet

If you were planning on buying your children a pet this Christmas, try adopting one instead. Animal shelters overflow with beautiful cats and dogs all year long, but especially during the holiday season. These animals usually have all their shots and vaccinations and even purebred pets are available from shelters, so in addition to being free, you'll be giving a healthy, loving animal a good home. Remember that animals need our charity, too.

Start a penny collection

This is a great activity for your kids. First, let them choose a place to donate their proceeds. Then help them create signs announcing the organization they are collecting for. If you prefer, call the organization and get a letter from them confirming your children's intentions. If your kids are teenagers, they can go door to door in your neighborhood or apartment building collecting everyone's pennies. Most people have a pile of pennies just sitting around collecting dust. This way they can get rid of the pesky coins and contribute to charity all at the same time! If your children are young, accompany them as you would on Halloween, and then teach them how to roll the coins into sleeves. Your kids will feel a real sense of achievement when they lug the money to the bank and then present the bills to their charity of choice.

Make a family scrapbook together

Here's a new idea for a holiday activity. Have each family member collect things that are important to them during the year—ticket stubs, photographs, newspaper clippings, awards or other kinds of memorabilia. Spend an afternoon choosing how to present all these items in a family scrapbook that will be a time capsule of the year. Keep all the scrapbooks together in one place in the house, and every year you can bring out the ones from years gone by. Soon you will find you have a new holiday tradition!

Donate unwanted or outgrown toys

Help your kids gather together any toys that they have outgrown that are still in good condition, and take your child with you when you donate them to a hospital or homeless shelter. If your kids receive toys during the year (birthday presents, etc.) that they already have or don't particularly want, save them for Christmastime and giftwrap them with your children before donating them. Some charities only accept new toys, so be sure to call first to find out the policy of your chosen charity.

Play parlor games

We didn't always have televisions and VCRs, and in Victorian times, Christmas offered the opportunity to play parlor games with family, friends, and neighbors. You already know how to play Charades and Twenty Questions, but you can add old favorites like Blind Man's Bluff, bridge, hearts, or any other card games to your repertoire. There is also an array of newer parlor games like Trivial Pursuit, Pictionary, and Balderdash! that are a lot of fun to play and are sure to bring people together. Playing games is a lot of fun and certainly more interactive than the latest video games or television shows. Parlor games stimulate your mind and can provide hours of family fun.

Ignore women's magazines during the holiday season

The easiest way to feel inadequate during the Christmas season is to read articles about how other people decorate their houses or celebrate the holiday. Ignore these articles! The people in them either have too much time on their hands or they are getting paid to create these wonderful Christmases. Women's magazines overflow with ideas for the most spectacular gingerbread house you've ever seen, decorating your home with evergreens, and the most beautiful cookies you can bake and hang on your tree. Forget it! Don't even buy the magazines! Don't watch Martha! You'll only feel bad. Some people have the time to spend weeks manufacturing a homemade Christmas that belongs in a magazine, but most of us don't. The idea is more Christmas spirit, not more Christmas cookies. Don't get caught up in someone else's homemade Christmas. Have your Christmas your way.

Perform random acts of kindness

Every day during the holiday season, perform one random act of kindness. Smile at a stranger, offer to help someone carry groceries to their car, volunteer at the library, give your old clothing to the Salvation Army, let someone get in front of you in line at the store, compliment a friend. There are always opportunities for these small, random acts of kindness, and they can do so much to brighten up the day—both yours and the other person's. Make it a habit that you can carry forward with you into the New Year. And make sure to share the stories with your family at dinnertime. Soon you will all be kinder and happier!

Give forgiveness to yourself and your loved ones

We all have spats, differences, and disagreements with friends and family. This holiday season, forgive someone you are angry with, and facilitate peace within your circle of family and friends. If you have two friends who aren't speaking to each other, invite them both out to lunch and get them talking again. Your good will can bring people together and bring yourself a better appreciation and understanding of the Christmas spirit.

Spend time with, not just money on, your kids

This year, make sure you spend more time with your children than you spend in the mall. As busy and responsible parents we have to shop, cook, and clean for the holidays in addition to fulfilling the social obligations of the season. There are holiday cocktail parties, office Christmas parties, and family parties. All in all, your children may begin to feel that they are last on your list. Some parents make it a policy to never go to a holiday party without their children. The holidays are for family, so any party that excludes children is probably not a true holiday party. So make a special effort to include them in all your Christmas plans. Your children will be happy you did.

Let the kids decorate this year

Instead of a fancy tree with expensive decorations, this year let the kids decorate. Let them make strings of cranberries, popcorn, or colorful breakfast cereals. Get lots of candy canes and tinsel and let them go to town on their own. Don't even try the kinds of Christmas lights that need every bulb tightened in order to light up—they're too hard to untangle anyway. Punch holes in Christmas cards and hang those on the tree, too. Decorating the tree can sometimes seem like too much of a chore, so if you feel this way, turn it over to the next generation and let them do whatever moves them. Have plenty of film on hand to record the event!

Plant trees instead of buying gifts

Planting a tree for someone is a lovely and lasting way to remind them of you. Most local and national parks have tree-planting programs. Donate trees for the people on your Christmas list, and be sure to send a card that lets them know about your gift on their behalf.

Talk about your family's Christmas expectations

Everyone has certain Christmas memories and rituals that they cherish, so have an open discussion with your family about which traditions are important to your holiday. Eliminate any that are unimportant or have lost their meaning for your family. Maybe your family doesn't want three different desserts for Christmas dinner but would be happy with ice cream and a store-bought cake. Involve everyone in these decisions so that no one feels disappointed or left out. If you want to simplify the holiday, you can find easy ways to do so, but make sure all are in agreement. A tradition that you think is unimportant or extravagant might be cherished by a spouse, in-law, or grandparent. Don't make scaling down the holiday a surprise: People need to know what to expect, and if you get them thinking that simpler is better, they're sure to think of different ways to bring out the simple spirit. It's okay to buy fewer gifts this year, as long as everyone knows there will be fewer packages under the tree before they arrive downstairs on Christmas morning.

Take a vacation day during the Christmas season

Take a day off and use it to do whatever *you* want to do most. You can use it to shop during the less-crowded hours or to get a massage, a facial, or a manicure. Take yourself out to a nice lunch, or meet some friends. See a movie. Buy *yourself* a Christmas present.

Another way is to spend this day in a way your children will enjoy: Play hooky with them. If school vacation hasn't yet begun, take them out of school and go do something fun together.

Make a family and friends cookbook

Starting several months before the holiday, ask family members and close friends for favorite recipes. The recipes can be either family traditions or simply a dish that person wants to share with other loved ones. Collect all of the recipes and add who contributed each recipe and why they especially like it. Make enough copies of each recipe for all the people who contributed and for others who might appreciate the collection. Bind them together in a loose-leaf notebook so that you can add new recipes each holiday season. This type of family and friends cookbook can be passed from one generation to another and is certain to be treasured by all.

Unplug the telephone on Christmas Day

This sounds a little radical, we know, but consider unplugging the telephone after you've made the necessary calls on Christmas morning. The constant ringing can seem jarring when you're trying to celebrate an old-fashioned holiday, and there probably isn't anyone you need to talk to on this special day. Make Christmas different by eliminating these kinds of distractions.

Celebrate the twelve days of Christmas

Don't pack all your Christmas activities and traditions into one day. Instead, spread them out over the traditional twelve days of Christmas and make the holiday a season rather than a one-day event. The whole family might want to volunteer for one day of charitable work or perhaps spend an evening addressing Christmas cards together. Go caroling in the neighborhood on another evening. Plan out a series of events that you can all partici-pate in together and set aside the time you need so you won't be interrupted. This shouldn't be a chore; the idea is to spread the Christmas spirit and joy around over several days instead of concentrating it into a few hours. Christmas will be more special for everyone this way.

Give family gifts

Often people give gifts to several members of the same family. This year, simplify your gift-giving by giving a family gift instead of individual ones. Buy the family a magazine subscription that everyone can enjoy, or give a video store membership, books they can all share, a computer game, a photo album, etc. Use your imagination and try to give something that the whole family can use. This is an easy way to substantially cut back on your gift list, and you'll save money at the same time.

Set a family spending limit

Get together and decide as a family how much you will spend on Christmas this year, and make no exceptions. People always spend more than they can afford, especially in those last few days before Christmas Day when you haven't yet found the perfect gift so you spend more to compensate. With a family spending limit, you'll know when to stop, and you'll be grateful in January when the bills begin to arrive.

Make your own wish list smaller by looking in your closet

At the beginning of the holiday season, clean out your closet. You'll find that you have many things you no longer need or wear, and you should donate all these items to the Salvation Army or to the thrift shop of your local hospital or favorite charitable organization. Pruning your closet accomplishes two important things: You will make a donation to charity, and you will realize how much you already have that you don't even need. The Christmas season often becomes a time of wanting and longing for things—that new chenille sweater, those gold earrings, or some other material thing. Coming face to face with how much you already own can be an eye-opening experience and can help you feel content with what you have. Maybe your own wish list will become a little smaller!

Cut back on Christmas cards

Before the mid-nineteenth century people wrote long holiday greetings to their friends and family. But in 1843, a London businessman named Henry Cole decided to ask his friend John Calcott Horseley to design an illustrated card that he could send out instead. Even then, most people were incredibly busy during the holiday! Christmas cards soon became all the rage, and today the average family sends out about forty cards every holiday season. That's forty cards to write personal notes in, address, stamp, and send in time for Christmas—right in the midst of all your other holiday preparations.

Are Christmas cards really necessary? It's up to you; some people are horrified at the idea of eliminating this tradition from their holidays. But if sending out Christmas cards has become a chore, we recommend that you simply forget about them and go on with your holiday. On the other hand, if you enjoy choosing exactly the right card each year, and if you use the opportunity to express your feelings for friends and family, then continue sending them. But cards that are sent with a greeting engraved that are simply signed by the sender don't

carry a great deal of affection with them. Think about what you want to do, and if you do decide to continue with the cards, at least take a good look at your list and prune it down to the people you care about most. You can choose three or four messages to send to different people—you wouldn't want two friends to receive exactly the same salutation! But if you have the time, it's much nicer to send a personal note or letter to each individual. Another way of handling this is to send out a newsletter to everyone on your list that lets them know what your family has been up to in the year gone by. Remember to personalize these a bit, too—it shows that you are really thinking about everyone on your list.

Make an extra turkey and give it away

If you're already cooking a turkey for Christmas dinner, roast an extra one and bring it to an organization or soup kitchen that serves holiday meals to the homeless. Cooking a turkey with all the fixings is a lot of work, but it's not much extra trouble to double the stuffing and throw in a second bird. You will enjoy your own meal much more when you know that others will not go hungry because of your generosity. Take the whole family with you to deliver the meal; this will let everyone share in the special feelings that are the true spirit of Christmas. Be sure to find out ahead of time when the organization is planning to serve their Christmas dinner!

Buy gifts from charitable organizations

When you purchase gifts from a nonprofit or charitable organization, you are actually giving twice. You benefit the charity you buy the gifts from, and of course the gift-recipient benefits, too. There are lots of interesting organizations that raise money with boutiques—call your local church, hospital, or community center to get some ideas.

Visit a local hospital or nursing home to sing carols on Christmas Eve

Don't forget that many people, often those without any family, must celebrate their Christmases from within the confines of a hospital room or a nursing home. Most of these places try to put on a Christmas celebration of their own, but they always enjoy having fresh faces to help out. If you like to go caroling in your neighborhood, try adding on a visit to a hospital, hospice, or nursing home. Many of them actually schedule groups of carolers to space out the visitors, so we suggest you call ahead to inquire about times you'll be welcome. You probably won't be able to see any stars since you'll be singing indoors, but the happiness you bring to the sick or elderly people around you will bring joy to your heart.

Make your own Christmas stockings

Like many of our Christmas traditions, the hanging of Christmas stockings probably comes from Victorian England. One story tells us that Father Christmas dropped some gold coins while making his way down a chimney, and they would have fallen through the grate and been lost forever if they hadn't landed in the stockings that had been hung up to dry. Ever since, children have hung their stockings with the hope that they will find them filled with coins or other gifts.

In our family, we used to fill stockings with small, inexpensive gifts that would fit into our stockings but were pretty useless. They might have been fun to receive on Christmas Day but they ended up as clutter later on. This year, instead of filling stockings with such knickknacks, give useful items such as pencils and pens, small kitchen utensils, magnets for the refrigerator, or even a deck of cards. These are just as much fun to open and they'll really be appreciated.

In most families everyone thinks about what to put in the Christmas stockings. This year think

about the stockings themselves. Make your own, either simply (such as with a new pair of heavy socks) or as a holiday craft project, with felt and glitter and anything else you can think of. Give the stockings as gifts!

Recycle gifts

Everyone has received gifts that they couldn't use—some nice place mats that don't match yours, bath oils, perfumed dusting powder, etc. They're probably sitting on a shelf in your linen closet. Gather them up, wrap them in pretty paper, and give them away. You can keep some on hand in case you need a last-minute gift for someone, or you can take them to a charity that will redistribute them to the needy.

Simplify your gift wrapping

Try buying pretty tissue paper in many different colors, or use brown craft paper, which you can buy in big rolls. You can personalize brown paper with ribbons in all colors, glitter, stickers, and rubber stamps instead of using store-bought wrapping paper, which is expensive. If you have small children, wrap gifts that are not fragile in brown paper and let them go to town decorating them with their own colorful artwork. Or give them large sheets of paper to paint and draw on before wrapping. Your gifts will certainly stand out and look unique under the tree!

People used to wrap gifts in white tissue paper tied with colored string until 1933, when wrapping paper on a roll was invented. By wrapping your gifts more plainly, you're actually going back to an older tradition.

Record a Christmas message

Make a cassette tape for family members or friends who live far away and can't make it home for Christmas. Have everyone in the family record their own greetings, and then add Christmas carols, a dramatic family reading of a favorite Christmas story, or anything else you can think of that will be appreciated by those you won't be seeing over the holiday. Unlike a phone call, the tape can be played over and over by the people you send it to, and it can be a great deal of fun to create.

Give homemade coupons instead of gifts

We shouldn't really say that coupons should be given *instead* of gifts, since gifts of service can be the greatest gifts of all. This year, make coupons for your friends and family, offering anything from a home-cooked meal to laundry service to a closet-cleaning session or a back or foot massage. You know which things will be most appreciated, and this type of gift is very personal and thoughtful, too. But you should keep in mind that the person receiving the coupon will be able to redeem it any time!

Have a tree-trimming party

Instead of working late into the night to decorate your own Christmas tree, make a party of it. Invite everyone you know to a tree-trimming party, and let them all contribute to your tree. Ask them to each bring an ornament, and in return you will give an ornament to everyone who comes. Make sure you have lots of eggnog and plenty of food on hand to feed all the busy decorators. This type of party is also terrific for small children, so that they don't feel left out of the festivities.

A newlyweds' first Christmas tree is often a little bare because they haven't had a chance to collect many ornaments. So instead of working late into the night to decorate on your own, or going out and spending a fortune to buy all new ornaments, make a party of it!

Have a potluck Christmas dinner

This year, tell each of your guests to bring one dish with them, and serve a potluck dinner for Christmas. Make sure you specify whether the guest should bring an appetizer, a main course dish, a side dish, or a dessert so that you don't end up with a table full of cakes and cookies but no vegetables! All you'll need to supply is the Christmas roast, whatever it may be. Having a potluck dinner is fun since you never know what will end up on your plate, and it's a great way to share all the food preparation without making your kitchen into a catering hall. Anyone who arrives without a dish must help you clean up!

Help your children give away their toys

This might seem like a strange suggestion at
Christmastime, we know, but it can be very effective
in teaching children about charity. Children often
want the latest advertised toys and can be insistent
that they receive a particular item or nothing at all.
Parents often trek from store to store in December,
searching for the right Power Ranger or other toy of
the moment. This year, try sitting down with your
child and going over his or her list for Santa together.
It's okay for your child to want specific things, but
you should try asking your child to give up one of
the toys that he or she already owns in exchange for
getting something new. But make sure your child
doesn't just offer up old or broken toys; rather, have
them choose a toy they will remember wishing for.
This is a good way to get children involved early on
in ideas about charity and the act of giving, and it
will also teach your child to think about which
things he or she really wants or needs. The child's
list of "must-have" toys will probably become smaller,
and you'll find fewer toys cluttering up your house,
abandoned and unused. Children are usually over-
loaded at Christmas—this pruning method will help
keep the number of toys under control.

Decorate with candles

Candles are a very symbolic and beautiful way to decorate at Christmastime. Long ago, tallow was used instead of the more expensive wax. But when wax became cheaper, candles became an emblem of Mary's purity, since wax is a product of virgin bees. Many ancient religious groups kept their own bees, and believed that bees came directly from heaven. It is said that the wax of a candle represents our body, the wick our soul, and the flame symbolizes our divine nature. The custom of placing lighted candles in the windows of a home began as a means of guiding travelers and Jesus. Candles are symbolic of Jesus, "Light of the World."

Pull back that rug and dance!

Instead of a formal sort of celebration, simply roll up the living room rug, put on your favorite music, and *dance!* Get the whole family on their feet, including the teenagers in your home, by asking them to choose some of the music. Don't let your grandmother sit idly by, either; make sure everyone takes a turn. Dancing is exhilarating, it's great exercise, and it will leave everyone breathless and wreathed in smiles. Dance as many nights as you can during the holidays, choosing a different sort of music each night. Invite over family and friends, and tell them to be sure to bring their dancing shoes!

Spread out your gift giving

If you have small children, they probably open their gifts in a frenzy on Christmas morning. All their anticipation for the holiday revolves around those few minutes, which go by all too quickly. Afterwards, everyone feels let down because the focal point of Christmas has already passed, leaving everyone feeling a bit underwhelmed.

Try gift giving a slightly different way this year. Instead of opening all the gifts at once, spread out this ritual over several days. Open a gift on Christmas Eve, a few on Christmas morning, another on the evening of Christmas Day, and one the day after Christmas. This way, the focus is not on a half hour of unwrapping presents, and the gifts are appreciated more when they're given out a few at a time.

Limit television during the entire month of December

Elsewhere in this book, we advise you to unplug your television on Christmas Day. But now we want to go a little further by advising you to set more stringent limits than usual during the holidays. Every hour of television during the months of November and December brings dozens and dozens of commercials for toys and other merchandise into your living room, creating an atmosphere of want, want, want. Limit your family's television viewing during the holidays and you may find that your kids are less obsessed with asking for the latest toys.

Bring back childhood Christmas traditions

Sit down with your spouse and your children, if they're old enough, and talk about your most cherished Christmas memories and traditions. Adults are now the givers of Christmas celebrations, rather than the recipients, as they were when they were children. This can make Christmas seem like an elaborate show staged for the next generation, and can leave the adults feeling a little hollow and unfulfilled inside. By incorporating the best traditions that you remember from your childhood, you can make Christmas more meaningful again. But be sure to include all adults in this discussion—everyone has very strong ideas about what Christmas should be, what it means to them, and you don't want anyone in your immediate family to feel left out or disappointed.

Take a Christmas stroll

Bundle up the whole family, including your pets, and take a walk around your neighborhood on the night of Christmas Eve. When you see everyone's lights burning and the glow of Christmas trees and candles behind the window drapes, you'll feel happy and warm inside. Indeed, there's something magical about Christmas Eve. Outside, it's crisp and clear and usually cold—the perfect time to sing carols or just to enjoy the silence of a winter's night.

Help children give gifts

Instead of just giving them gifts, take your kids shopping for gifts for needy kids. Children are more likely to appreciate receiving gifts if they learn also to give them. Let them wrap the gifts and place them under the tree with the understanding that Santa can take gifts to give to other children as well as leaving them for your kids.

Give ornaments for the tree as presents

Everyone likes to have ornaments that they can treasure year after year. Ornaments make good family gifts, and they are also nice gifts for your spouse or your children. Kids can make their own ornaments out of baker's clay and hang them on the tree themselves. These can be their gifts to you!

RECIPE FOR BAKER'S CLAY
Ingredients:
2 cups flour
1 cup salt
1 cup water
2 tablespoons oil

Directions:
Mix all ingredients together, and knead until smooth. Roll out the dough to about ¼ inch thick and use cookie cutters or a dull knife to cut the ornaments into shapes. Bake on a cookie sheet at 350°F until dry (about 15 minutes). After they cool, decorate ornaments with paints, glitter, etc. If you plan to hang the ornaments, insert a paper clip in the top of the ornament before baking in the oven. And remember to credit the artist and the year of the creation on the back of each!

Decorate your home simply

In Victorian times people decorated their homes
for the holiday by bringing in sprigs of evergreens.
Even well before the Christian era, evergreens were
a symbol of eternal life because while cold weather
killed most plants, evergreens survived. Many people
used to believe that evergreen trees shielded them
from evil spirits. You can decorate your halls with
boughs of evergreen and holly—simple, natural
ways to bring the beauty of the outdoors into your
home. To the Druids, holly's green, shiny leaves
proved that the sun never left the earth. A bit of
holly was placed on a bedpost to bring on pleasant
dreams; placed on a house it warded off witches.
Keep ill spirits away from your house by using lots
of it—and remember to place some mistletoe over
doorways, where it is certain to inspire many affec-
tionate kisses!

Start a journal of family thanksgiving

Buy a notebook or a journal for your family to share. When something wonderful happens to or for a family member during the coming year, encourage them to record the happy event, or you can write it up for them. People tend to dwell always on what went wrong, or on criticism they received, or on a promise that wasn't kept. By chronicling more pleasant moments, whether they are as simple as a compliment, or as major as a new job, a raise, or the birth of a child, you can keep track of all the many good things that happen throughout the year. At the end of next year, make it a new Christmas tradition to read aloud from your family journal in order to relive all the happy times you've experienced together.

Keep travel to a minimum

It seems that everyone is always rushing to get somewhere else in time for Christmas Eve instead of going home and relaxing. If you enjoy Christmas most when you celebrate it at another home, by all means go ahead and make your travel plans (but do it early). But if traveling has become a big hassle, with the kids fighting all the way in the backseat of the car, then try the holiday at home this year. You can invite your extended family and friends to join yours this year, or just make it a small gathering of immediate family members. You don't have to look for Christmas spirit only in a crowd; Christmas is where *you* make it.

Don't buy tabletop decorations

Instead of purchasing fancy linens and napkins and centerpieces for your holiday table, decorate simply this year. Use bits of ribbon instead of napkin rings for a festive look, and pile the center of the table with pine cones, holly, and fresh fruit, such as apples, oranges, pears, and pomegranates. Your table will look homemade, and no one will sit down afraid to touch anything! Apples are customarily eaten at Christmastime for good luck, so be sure to include them in your fruit centerpieces. If you have pretty trays or silver platters, use them as the foundation for your creations.

Keep a few extra gifts around the house

In this book, we've tried to de-emphasize presents because we don't believe that gifts should be the center around which the holiday revolves. But inevitably you will forget to put someone on your list who hasn't forgotten you, and if you have extra gifts in the closet that you can pull out in a pinch, you can save yourself a lot of guilt and some last-minute shopping frenzy. Wrap them up beforehand, and remember to keep aside some extra gift cards, and you'll be all set for any unexpected surprises. Keep the gifts simple, and make them things that you can give to anyone—picture frames, board games, or books. That way they'll be sure to be appreciated, even if you don't know who will receive them beforehand!

Rent Christmas movies to put yourself in the holiday mood

Whenever the season begins to feel like a hassle, get yourself back in the right mood by renting one of the classic Christmas movies that is guaranteed to put it all in perspective again. Whether you choose *It's a Wonderful Life* or *A Christmas Carol* or even *How the Grinch Stole Christmas*, you'll feel much better. Here's a list of some of our favorites, just to get you started:

Babes in Toyland
A Christmas Carol
The Christmas That Almost Wasn't
Dr. Seuss's How the Grinch Stole Christmas
Home Alone
It Happened One Christmas
It's a Wonderful Life
Miracle on 34th Street
The Muppet Christmas Carol
National Lampoon's Christmas Vacation
The Night Before Christmas
The Nutcracker
Scrooged
A Very Brady Christmas
Yes, Virginia, There Is a Santa Claus

Remember your pets

Pets like presents too, so don't forget yours. Some families like to give their pet a new bed or pretty water bowl at Christmastime, and all pets appreciate the gesture. Pets also enjoy new toys, like stuffed animals or squeaky rubber toys. Catnip and rawhide bones are beloved by cats and dogs, respectively. Remember to wrap a present for your pet and to reward him for all his loyalty and love in the past year. And don't forget those leftovers from Christmas dinner!

Celebrate Los Posados

Los Posados is a Mexican Christmas festival that takes place between December 16th and 25th. This holiday reenacts Joseph and Mary's search for an inn in which to sleep on each of nine nights. Different families invite other villagers in for an evening of song, dance, food, and piñatas. You can celebrate by inviting your neighbors in on the nights before Christmas to share in some of the simple merrymaking at your home. You can even make it into a block party! In Mexico, the tradition calls for half of the families to play the innkeepers and for the other half to play Mary and Joseph searching for a place to sleep. You can adapt this lovely celebration and create an entirely new way of enjoying the nights before Christmas.

Give away a Christmas plate

Follow the Danish tradition of giving away a Christmas plate. When the Danes gave away food during the holidays, they placed it on a special plate that they had decorated just for the holiday— they painted it with holiday motifs. People collected these plates over the years (and still do) and used them every holiday season to display and serve their Christmas sweets. You can find pretty plates at flea markets and garage sales, china dishes that were once part of a beautiful set, and use them to give away your special, homebaked cakes and cookies. Remember, you should only find yourself baking if it's something you really enjoy doing—otherwise, store-bought treats are always good enough.

Be a clown for a day

During the Christmas season there are always many despondent children sick in the hospital, missing their Christmas tree, their family celebrations, and their traditional Christmas dinners. You can brighten up a child's day by dressing up as a clown and visiting the pediatric ward of your local hospital. Bring some cookies (check with the nurses first to make sure they're allowed), some bright balloons, and some makeup that you can use to paint their faces. Also remember to take a couple of cheery children's books to read aloud—the smiles you see will warm the very cockles of your heart, no matter how cold the climate you live in.

Organize your own family charity

At the beginning of each year, make a piggy bank and put it in a place, such as the kitchen, where all the family members can see it all the time. This is now a place for Dad to put all his spare change each night, for the kids to contribute part of their allowance each week, and for Mom to put in her part. At the beginning of December, the family should sit down together to count up how much money is in the bank and then to decide how it should be given away. Especially at the end of the year, most people are besieged with requests for charitable donations, so you can choose one of those or a favorite charity. Just as a real foundation works, your family foundation can give to one charity or to several—but the idea is that the whole family should decide together how the money is given away. This will help teach children how important it is to think of those less fortunate than themselves.

Create your own loop
of Christmas music

Everyone enjoys holiday music, but most people have only an album or two of traditional Christmas songs. Instead of keeping your radio on all day, borrow Christmas albums from your friends and make your own cassette of holiday music that you can play as often and for as long as you want. It will have your personal favorites, the songs your children always ask for, and it can quickly become one of the traditions you look forward to each year. If your children are old enough, ask them to participate, too—kids often like to record music. And your family's holiday collection can also make a nice homemade gift to give away to your family friends.

Go and see The Nutcracker

Take your entire family to see a local production of *The Nutcracker*. This is an incredibly beautiful ballet, and most of the music will be familiar and beloved by everyone. Almost every town offers a local performance; if yours doesn't, you can even rent it on video or make a point of recording the PBS version that is shown every year, to play back when the whole family is together. Some of our earliest Christmas memories are of going to New York City to see this ballet, and to this day the music is powerfully evocative.

Perform a Christmas skit with your family

This is an activity that the whole family can participate in and enjoy to the hilt. As a family, decide on the skit you want to perform, and then work on putting it together for a performance on Christmas Day, maybe right after dinner. Religious plays were part of the medieval Christmas tradition and still are performed in many countries. You can reenact the coming of the Magi, or three kings, or you can perform A *Christmas Carol*. You'll find that it brings out the amateur actor in each of you!

Answer a child's letter

This is an opportunity for you to become Santa
Claus for a day, although the feeling you get will last
a lifetime. All post offices collect children's letters
to Santa Claus, and usually a local organization will
try to match these letters with a patron who wants
to make a child's wish come true. You can either
volunteer to work in the organization's office, or,
if you can afford it, you can grant a wish that is
within your budget. Some of the wishes are modest,
others are impossible to meet ("please make my
mother all better"), but you can certainly bring
Santa Claus to the home of a needy or lonely child
this Christmas.

Have your holiday meal in a restaurant this year

Many people enjoy cooking a big, elaborate Christmas dinner, but there are just as many who would rather leave the ordeal to others. If you haven't been invited to someone else's home for the holiday, consider taking your family out for Christmas dinner instead of spending the entire day and evening in the kitchen, cooking and then cleaning up. It's true that your options for dining out are somewhat limited on the holiday, but if you don't mind having Chinese food or another exotic cuisine instead of the traditional turkey and all its trimmings, eating out can be great fun, and a change of pace.

Create your own prayer book

Collect prayers (they can be from your own religion only or they can be from any religion) that you find especially meaningful or lovely in some way, and make them into a little booklet that you can enjoy alone or share with the rest of your family and friends. If you like, you can ask them for contributions of prayers that are significant for them, too. But the idea is that this is a personal prayer book—a way of personalizing the meaning of a holiday that can sometimes be lost in lengthy church services.

Trade vacation days with someone at work

If your workplace doesn't close for Christmas, find someone who celebrates a different holiday and offer to switch vacation days with them. That way, each of you can have off the day that is most meaningful for you, and your boss won't be left shorthanded.

Give homemade gifts this year

People tend to go overboard with their gift buying at Christmas, and in this book we've tried to encourage you to cut back. One way you might do this is by making it a family rule to *make* your gifts instead of buying them. Since this entails a lot of work (and a great deal of love!), it automatically places the emphasis where it belongs—on the thought and not on the gift. You don't have to make the gifts elaborate—a simple knitted scarf, a painting or drawing, or a sachet to keep drawers smelling sweet. The idea is to craft something rather than purchasing it outright. This will also limit the number of gifts you can give to people, again making Christmas more about people than about what you are giving to them or receiving from them.

Have a Christmas picnic!

Here's an idea for those of you who live in warm climates: Make Christmas dinner a Christmas picnic this year. Picnics are a great way to bring together friends and family; you can invite as many people as you like without the cooking becoming a chore; and there's almost no cleanup required. Ask your guests to bring their own baskets and blankets, or have them bring their own chicken or hamburgers and you can simply supply the barbecue. Picnics are the best excuse to share in games or storytelling. Even if you live where there is snow, you can still picnic indoors if the idea appeals to you. Invite your friends and family to bring a blanket and their own picnic basket, and clear out all the furniture from your living room. You can picnic right at home; this kind of party will surely be a novelty.

Limit alcohol at holiday meals and parties

To simplify holiday cocktail parties, consider offering your guests only eggnog or wine instead of feeling the need to offer a complete bar. Most people will never notice the difference, and you should spend your time enjoying the party rather than mixing drinks. Set up a simple self-service bar with a couple of choices, and let your guests serve themselves.

During holiday meals, limit the amount of alcohol you pass around the table; anyone should be able to celebrate without overdoing it. We all know the feeling of being hung over on Christmas Day because we had too much to eat and drink the night before. This year, keep it light, and keep it sober—you'll find you can enjoy everything much more clearly that way!

Attend midnight Mass

Midnight Mass is one of the most beautiful ceremonies, and going to church late at night with your entire family brings a special religious element back into a holiday that can easily be over-commercialized.

After the Mass, come home to the French tradition of *le reveillon*, which is a special late supper. The menu for this meal changes depending on which region of France you are in, but it always includes the traditional Yule log–shaped cake called the *buche de Noël*.

Don't forget Santa Claus

Some parents are uncertain about how long they should allow their children to believe in Santa Claus. Usually it's the oldest child in the family who tells her siblings that Santa Claus doesn't exist. But Santa Claus embodies the very spirit of Christmas, and so he is real enough for all of us. We believe that children should experience their childhoods, and live their childhood dreams and fantasies, as long as they can—and this means keeping Santa Claus very much alive in their hearts. Make a point of setting out some milk and cookies for your ruddy visitor, in case he gets hungry during his travels. Your kids will delight in being able to offer something back to Santa, and you'll have a little snack to nibble on late at night after you've finished putting all the gifts under the tree!

Share other religions with your children

Invite someone who celebrates a holiday other than Christmas to share in your holiday celebration, and ask them to talk to your children about their beliefs. Christmas is a good time for children to learn about Hanukkah and Kwanzaa, and it's important for them to realize that different people celebrate their special holidays in different ways. If you don't know anyone to invite, check some books out of your local library and educate yourself and your family about our world's cultures and religious traditions.

We hope that you have enjoyed this little book, and that it has given you the inspiration to enjoy a simpler Christmas this year. We would like to hear about other ways that you may have discovered to bring the spirit back into the Christmas holiday, so please write to us in care of our publisher at:

Andrews McMeel Publishing
4520 Main Street
Kansas City, MO 64111-7701

Happy Holidays!